Pepperoni Cookies

Fearful Fergus Learns to TRY

Written by Sarah Chaires

Illustrated by Elizabeth Tortora

Pepperoni Cookies

Fearful Fergus Learns to Try

Text Copyright © 2024 Sarah Chaires
Illustrations Copyright © 2024 Elizabeth Tortora
All rights reserved.
Independently Published by BiblioKid Publishing.
PO BOX 512, Ankeny, IA 50021

www.bibliokidpublishing.com

www.fergusthemastiff.com

ISBN: Paperback - 978-1-955767-59-0
Ebook - 978-1-955767-61-3

Author's Dedication:

*To my family & friends who
have supported and loved me
during my breast cancer journey!
Thank you!*

BOOM!

The thunder **CRASHED!** Fergus **shivered**. He hated storms.

Fergus wanted to **SNUGGLE** his mom,
but she was...
upstairs.

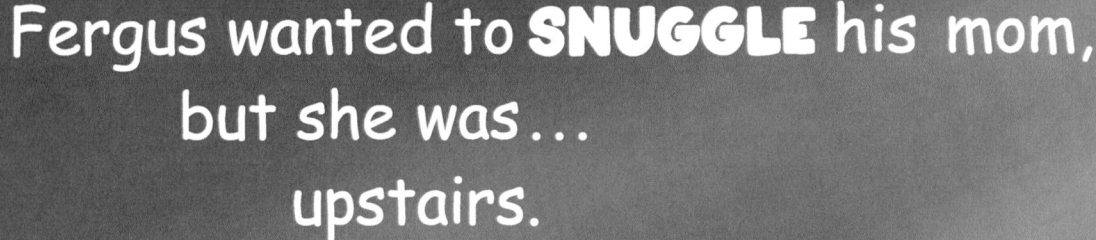

"Come on, Fergus. You can snuggle with me upstairs!" his mom called.

Fergus

looked up the

sky-scraping stairs...

He had to try,

but . . . he was **petrified** to try new things.

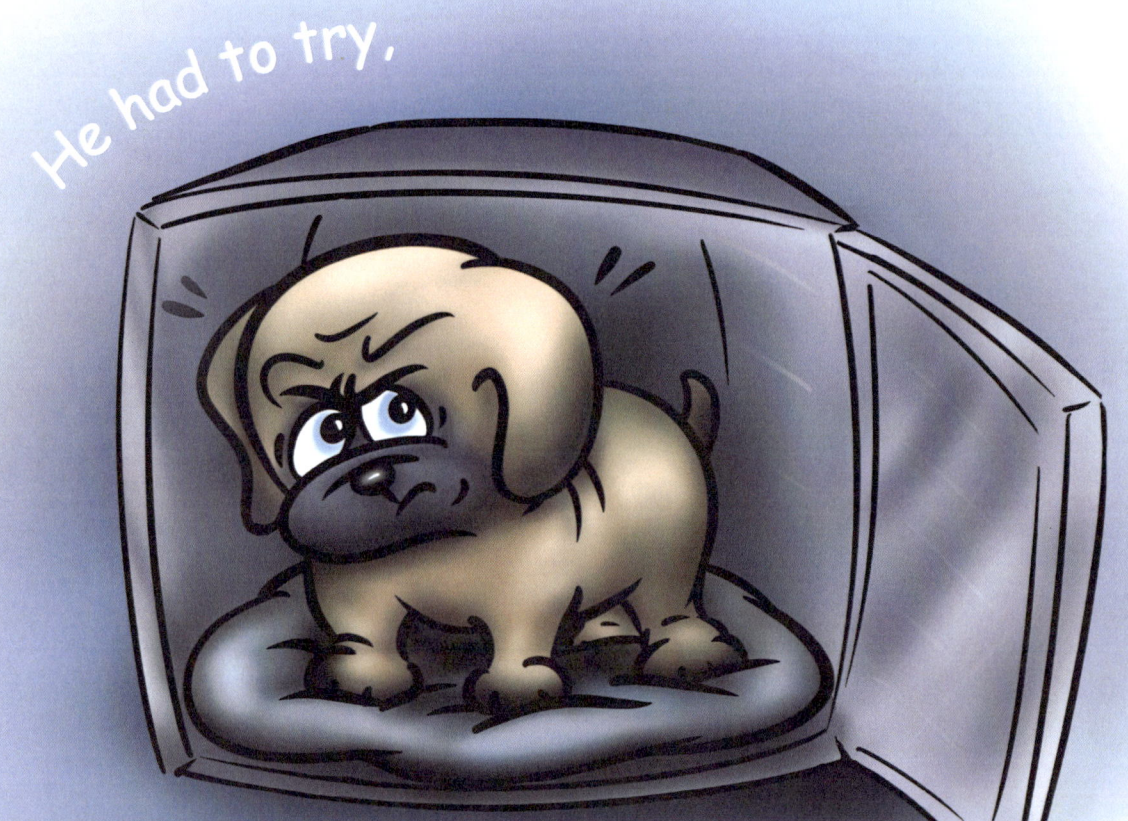

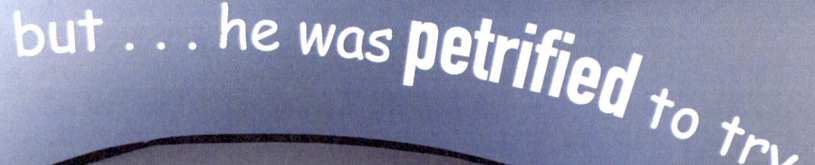

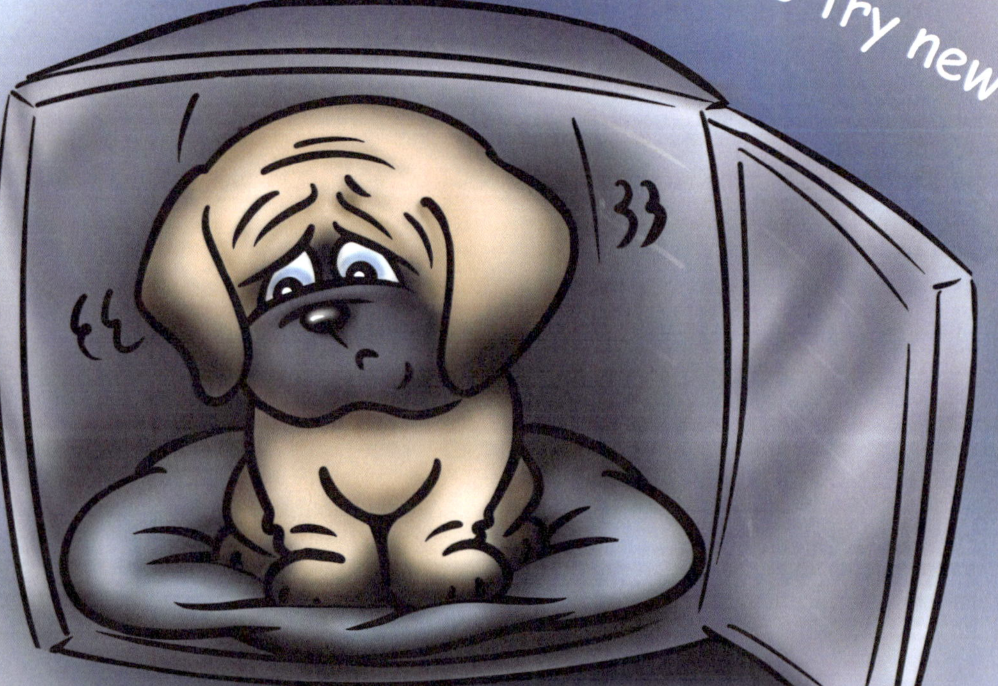

Just then, something **tickled** his nose.

The **sweetest**, most **savory** smell in the whole world!

PEPPERONI COOKIES!

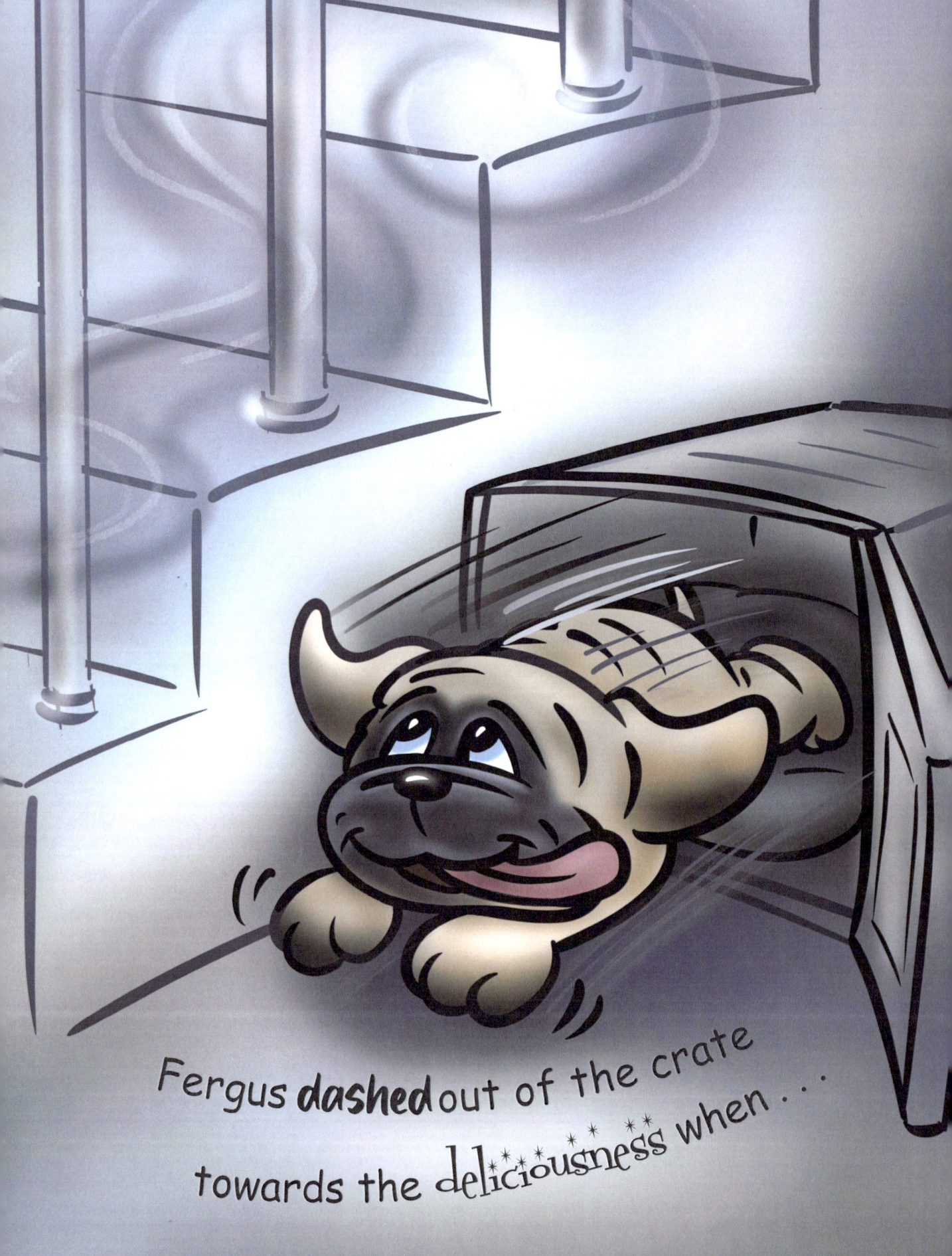

He spotted the first cookie on the first stair.

He puppy-pondered the risks and the rewards of climbing the stairs.

If he **slipped**,

With a quick **slurp** of the tongue, he **gobbled** up the first pepperoni cookie.

The baked treat warmed his tummy. He thought of returning to the safety of his crate, but the sweet smell of the deliciousness filled his nose again.

Could he really climb to the top of the towering stairs? **He had to try.** At least, to save the cookies.

Fergus slurped up the second pepperoni cookie, then pounced on the third. Honing in on the next prize, he leapt onto the next step ...

and the next ... until...

KER-BOOM!

The thunder blasted.

Fergus' legs wobbled like the trees in the wind.
He dug his paws into the wood and gripped for life.
Maybe it was safer in the crate.

His mom was counting on him.
He didn't want to fail.
He had to try.
Fergus reached out
his front paw.
His back paws started to slip,
stretched out
between two stairs.

BA-BOOM!

The house shook from the thunder. Then . . .

ALL of Fergus's paws slipped.
Fergus tumbled
all
the
way
down
the stairs . . .

KER-SPLAT!

Fergus laid on his belly, flattened like a pancake.
Maybe he shouldn't have tried.

"Fergus, you can do it!
You just need to try!"
His mom's voice
echoed down the steps.
Fergus refused to move,
his pride bruised.
Once again, he peered up
the sky-scraping stairs.
With a deep inhale,
the sweet savory smell of
the pepperoni cookies
called to him.
He had to try,
one final time.

This time when Fergus extended his paw — no wobbles!

Slurp, slurp,

slurp!

He hopped up the stairs as quick as a bunny, **WOOFING** down the sweet pepperoni cookies with each step.
His paws pranced upwards, until . . .

Fergus finally reached the top!
Like an owl perched with pride
overlooking his new horizon,
Fergus gazed down
the steep stairs.

He had conquered the pepperoni cookie mountain! "I knew you could do it, Fergus!" his mom cheered. "You just needed pepperoni cookies to try!"

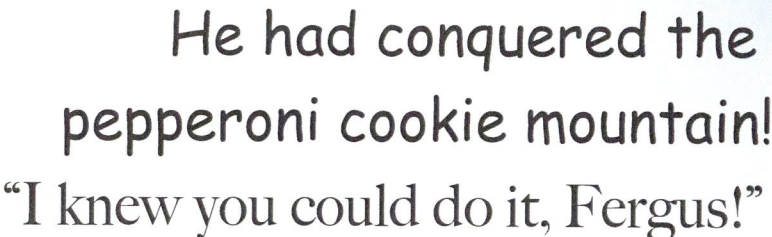

Fergus snuggled with his mom
in bed, cozy and safe.
Full of love and pepperoni cookies,
Fergus dreamed about all the
new things he could try . . .
with pepperoni cookies, of course.

Pepperoni Cookies Recipe *by Chef Jason Lawless*

(Made for people, but safe for dogs)

Prep time: 20 min
Total time: 30 min
Servings: 36 cookies

Ingredients for the Cookies:
1 1/2 cups sugar
1/2 cup butter, softened at room temperature
1/2 cup shortening
2 eggs
2 3/4 cups flour
2 tsp cream of tartar
1 tsp baking soda
1 tsp ground cinnamon
1 pack (4 oz.) diced pepperoni

Ingredients for the Glaze:
2 Tbsp salted butter
1/4 cup pure maple syrup
3/4 cup powdered sugar
1/2 tsp vanilla extract
a pinch of salt

1. Heat oven to 400°F.
2. Mix the sugar, butter, shortening, and eggs in a large bowl.
3. Stir in flour, cream of tartar, baking soda, cinnamon, and salt. Mix well.
4. Roll the dough into balls (about 1/4–1/3 inch each) and place them on an ungreased baking sheet, 2 inches apart.
5. Press a pinch of diced pepperoni into the top of each of the balls.
6. Bake 9–11 minutes.
7. Let the cookies cool on a cooling rack before glazing.

To prepare the glaze:
Microwave the butter and maple syrup in a microwave safe bowl until melted. Then whisk in the powdered sugar, vanilla extract, and pinch of salt until smooth. Adjust powdered sugar as needed to get a good glaze consistency. Drizzle over the room temperture cookies using a spoon or a piping bag.

For the dog's recipe, please visit
www.fergusthemastiff.com

Authors Note

This story is based on the true life events of Fergus, a real-life 250-pound English Mastiff.
His full American Kennel Club (AKC) title is:
Grand Champion HarvestHaze Fergus of The Sand Dunes.
He is a top-ranked AKC Conformation show dog in the United States.

About the Author

Sarah Chaires is a Medical Provider and founder of a non-profit that provides educational opportunities for children in foster care. She and her husband are proud parents of three wonderful sons. Sarah is a Breast Cancer survivor. She and her family believe that the combination of self-confidence, love, and determination creates the ultimate superpower that catapults one to success . . . and it all starts with "YOU CAN DO IT!"

About the Illustrator

Elizabeth worked in advertising and toy design after graduating in graphic design from Parsons in NYC. But she always secretly wanted to be a children's book illustrator, as she loves to express herself in fun and whimsical ways. After having two daughters, she and her family moved to North Carolina, adopted two dogs, and shortly after began a pet portrait business. When her friend, Sarah, told her about her idea for a children's book series that dealt with the common emotional struggles young children endure, but seeing it through the eyes of a dog, Elizabeth was enthusiastic. She knew from watching her own kids the many ways in which children can relate and learn from their pets. Elizabeth hopes these books not only bring comfort and understanding, but also laughter and fun.

Printed in the USA
CPSIA information can be obtained
at www.ICGtesting.com
JSRC082342270324
59920JS00007B/21